The World SERIES

All About Pro Baseball's
Biggest Event

by Hans Hetrick

CAPSTONE PRESS
a capstone imprint

Sports Illustrated Kids Winner Takes All is published by Capstone Press,
1710 Roe Crest Drive, North Mankato, Minnesota 56003.
www.capstonepub.com

Library of Congress Cataloging-in-Publication Data
Hetrick, Hans, 1973–
    The World Series : all about pro baseball's biggest event / by Hans Hetrick.
    p. cm.—(Edge books)
    Includes bibliographical references and index.
    Summary: "Describes MLB's World Series championship, including some of the
greatest teams, players, and moments from World Series history"—Provided by publisher.
    ISBN 978-1-4296-6574-2 (library binding)
    ISBN 978-1-4296-9444-5 (paperback)
    1. World Series (Baseball)—Juvenile literature. I. Title.
GV878.4.H48 2013
796.357'646—dc23   2011048898

Editorial Credits

Aaron Sautter, editor; Heidi Thompson, designer; Eric Gohl, media researcher;
    Laura Manthe, production specialist

Photo Credits

Dreamstime: Imdan, cover, 1 (trophy); Getty Images: B. Bennett, 24;
Library of Congress: 25; Newscom: Zuma Press/Keystone, 7; NY Daily
News Archive via Getty Images: 23; Sports Illustrated: Al Tielemans,
cover (background), 3, 8, David E. Klutho, 4, 14, 15, Heinz Kluetmeier,
12, 13, 29, John Biever, cover (left & right), 21, John D. Hanlon, 20, John G
Zimmerman, 18, John Iacono, 19, 26, 27, 28, V.J. Lovero, 17, Walter
Iooss Jr., cover (middle), 10, 11, 16

Design Elements

iStockphoto: Shane Martin; Shutterstock: MaxyM,
Redshinestudio, rendergold

Records listed in this book are current as of the 2011 season.

Printed in the United States of America in Stevens Point, Wisconsin.
032013   007240R

· TABLE OF CONTENTS ·

The Fall Classic

David Freese

A red sea of Cardinals fans stood nervously in the stands. David Freese, the third baseman for the St. Louis Cardinals, stepped into the batter's box. It was the bottom of the 11th inning in Game 6 of the 2011 World Series.

The Texas Rangers led the series three games to two. The Cardinals needed a win to keep their championship hopes alive. When Freese swung at the next pitch, he crushed the ball over the centerfield fence. A roar erupted from the fans at Busch Stadium and across St. Louis.

The Cardinals had twice been one strike away from defeat. But Freese's home run had won the game to send the Series to Game 7. St. Louis manager Tony La Russa tried to explain the Cardinals' Game 6 miracle. He said, "What happened today, I just think, you had to be there to believe it."

The World Series is often called the Fall Classic. The best-of-seven series features two of the best teams in Major League Baseball (MLB). The World Series has delivered thrills like David Freese's game-winning home run for more than 100 years.

LIVING ON THE EDGE

The amazing Game 6 win was not the first surprise of the Cardinals' 2011 season. On August 24 St. Louis was 10½ games behind in the standings. But the team made a late season push to win 23 of its last 32 games. The Cardinals claimed the National League wild card spot on the last day of the season.

BIRTH OF THE WORLD SERIES

In 1903 the Pittsburgh Pirates had a huge lead in the National League (N.L.) In the American League (A.L.), teams couldn't keep up with the Boston Pilgrims. At that time, the N.L. and A.L. never played each other. But many baseball fans wondered what would happen if each league's best teams faced each other.

The Pittsburgh Pirates' owner, Barney Dreyfuss, saw a great opportunity. He wrote a letter to the Boston Pilgrims' owner, Henry Killilea. Dreyfuss suggested they organize a World Series. He believed a matchup between the two teams would be a great success. Killilea agreed, and they made plans for the first World Series.

The World Series was an instant hit. The first game was played on October 1, 1903. More than 16,000 fans squeezed into Boston's tiny Huntington Avenue Baseball Grounds. The Pilgrims won the first World Series Championship five games to three.

TRIPLE THE FANS

The first World Series was extremely popular. Fans who couldn't find a seat in Boston's small ballpark stood in the outfield grass. Balls hit into the fans were considered ground rule triples. There were a record 25 triples hit in the 1903 World Series.

The San Francisco Giants celebrated at the pitcher's mound after winning the 2010 World Series.

THE ROAD TO THE TITLE

The World Series has always been a matchup between the A.L. and N.L. pennant winners. But over the years, the way teams get to the World Series has changed. In 1903 there were only 16 MLB teams. As the league grew, the road to the World Series became longer.

At first the World Series was the only postseason series. But in 1969 MLB expanded to 24 teams. Each league was split into two divisions. The two division champions in each league played in the A.L. and N.L. Championship Series. Then the pennant winners played in the World Series.

In 1994 MLB added a third division to each league and a second round of playoffs. A third round of playoffs was added in 2012. Today six division winners and four wild card teams advance to the playoffs. In the first round, the wild card teams meet in a single playoff game. The winners advance to a best-of-five Division Series. The winners of those series then play in the A.L. and N.L. Championship Series to compete for a pennant. Finally, the two league champs play for the World Series title.

MOST WORLD SERIES CHAMPIONSHIPS

Team	Championships
NEW YORK YANKEES	27
ST. LOUIS CARDINALS	11
OAKLAND ATHLETICS	9
BOSTON RED SOX	7
SAN FRANCISCO GIANTS	7

Historic Series

The greatest World Series are filled with suspense. One pitch, one swing, or one catch can make the difference between winning and losing. Game 7 is often the most memorable game, but sometimes Game 6 features the greatest drama in baseball.

1975 - Cincinnati Reds vs. Boston Red Sox

In the 1975 World Series, Game 6 was a baseball fan's dream. The game featured dramatic home runs and game-saving catches. The Cincinnati Reds led the series three games to two. In the bottom of the 12th inning, the score was tied 6-6.

LET'S PLAY NINE

In 1903, 1919, 1920, and 1921, the World Series was a best-of-nine series. Every other World Series has featured a best-of-seven playoff.

Cincinnati Reds great Pete Rose

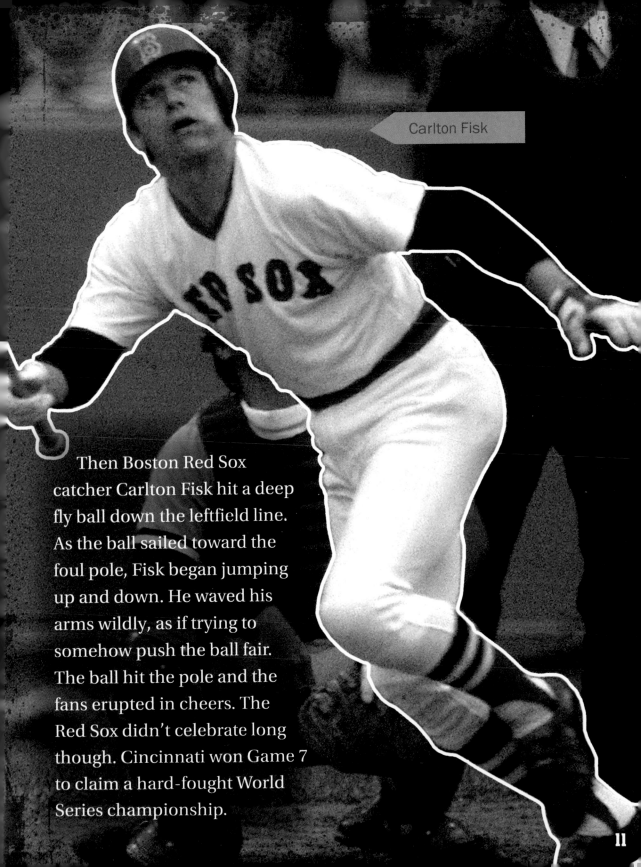

Then Boston Red Sox catcher Carlton Fisk hit a deep fly ball down the leftfield line. As the ball sailed toward the foul pole, Fisk began jumping up and down. He waved his arms wildly, as if trying to somehow push the ball fair. The ball hit the pole and the fans erupted in cheers. The Red Sox didn't celebrate long though. Cincinnati won Game 7 to claim a hard-fought World Series championship.

1991 - Minnesota Twins vs. Atlanta Braves

In 1990 the Atlanta Braves and the Minnesota Twins each finished at the bottom of their divisions. But in 1991 both teams rocketed from worst to first. After advancing in the first two playoff rounds, they faced off in one of the most dramatic World Series in history. Five of the seven games were decided by just one run. Three games went into extra innings.

By Game 6 the Braves led the Series 3-2. In the bottom of the 11th inning, the game was tied 3-3 when the Twins' Kirby Puckett came up to bat. Puckett took a few pitches before hitting a big game-winning homer to force Game 7.

Game 7 was an amazing pitchers' duel between the Braves' John Smoltz and the Twins' Jack Morris. For eight innings the two pitchers put zeroes on the scoreboard.

Jack Morris

The Braves relieved Smoltz in the eighth inning. But Morris stayed on the mound and kept throwing shutout baseball.

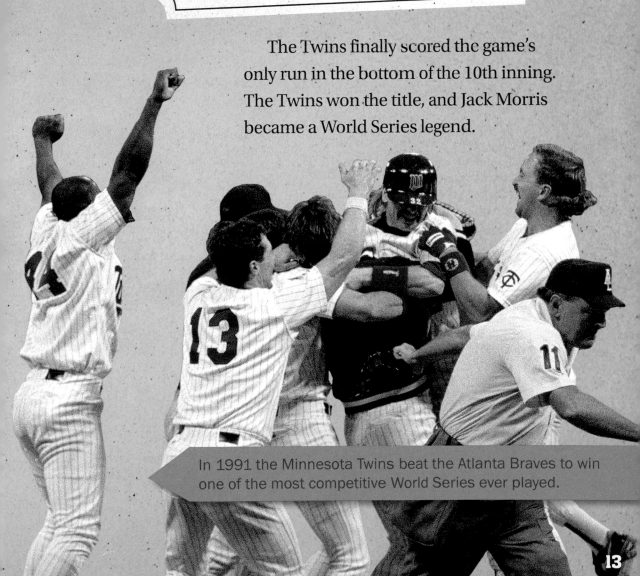

The Twins finally scored the game's only run in the bottom of the 10th inning. The Twins won the title, and Jack Morris became a World Series legend.

In 1991 the Minnesota Twins beat the Atlanta Braves to win one of the most competitive World Series ever played.

2011 - St. Louis Cardinals vs. Texas Rangers

In 2011 the St. Louis Cardinals almost missed their chance at history. The team barely squeaked into the playoffs. Then the Cardinals continued their unlikely run to the World Series by beating two heavily favored teams—the Philadelphia Phillies and Milwaukee Brewers.

But the Cardinals' luck nearly ran out in Game 6—twice! The Texas Rangers led the Series 3-2 and were hungry for their first championship. In the bottom of the ninth inning, the Rangers were ahead 7-5. The Cardinals had two outs, and the batter, David Freese, had two strikes. But then he smacked a triple into rightfield to tie the game.

In the 10th inning, the Rangers took back the lead with a two-run homer. The Cardinals were once again one strike away from defeat when Lance Berkman drove in the tying run. Then in the 11th inning, Freese won Game 6 with a heroic **walk-off home run**.

Lance Berkman

walk-off home run—a game-winning home run in the bottom of the last inning of a game

The dramatic Game 6 win kept the Cardinals in the series. St. Louis kept the momentum going and beat the Rangers 6-2 in Game 7 to win the championship. The Cardinals' surprising title run made the 2011 World Series one of the most dramatic in history.

St. Louis surprised many baseball fans by winning the 2011 World Series.

17

Heroes of October

World Series heroes aren't always an ace pitcher or home run king. The list of heroic players includes all types, from All-Stars to rookies. It's impossible to predict who will be the next hero. It's just another reason the World Series is so fun to watch.

Reggie Jackson

CHAPTER 3

REGGIE'S THREE

In 1977 one of the greatest World Series performances was put on by "Mr. October" himself—Reggie Jackson. In the fourth inning of Game 6, the Yankees slugger began an incredible run against the Dodgers. First he hit a two-run homer off Burt Hooton's first pitch. Then in the fifth inning, Jackson hit Elias Sosa's first pitch out of the park. In the eighth inning, he smacked another first-pitch homer, this time against Charlie Hough. In three straight at bats, Jackson smashed home runs on the first pitch. "There's a ballplayer in me that responds to all that pressure," Jackson said. "I'm not sure that I hit three homers today, but the ballplayer in me did."

SERIES STREAKS

Between 1949 and 1953, the New York Yankees won a record five straight World Series titles. The Yankees had previously won four straight championships between 1936 and 1939. The Oakland Athletics won three straight between 1972 and 1974. Then the Yankees had another three-title streak from 1998 to 2000.

Derek Jeter was a key part of the Yankees' success in the late 1990s.

LIVING THE DREAM

Every ballplayer dreams of winning a championship with a walk-off home run. But in more than 100 years, only two players have lived baseball's ultimate fantasy.

By Game 7 of the 1960 World Series, the Pittsburgh Pirates and New York Yankees each had three wins. In the bottom of the ninth inning, the game was tied when the Pirates' Bill Mazeroski came to the plate. He was known more for his great defensive play than for his hitting. But he slammed the first championship-winning walk-off homer in World Series history. When he realized he had won the World Series, he leaped for joy and threw his arms in the air. His teammates swarmed around him at home plate to celebrate the title.

MOST CAREER WORLD SERIES · HOME RUNS ·

MICKEY MANTLE • NEW YORK YANKEES	18
BABE RUTH • NEW YORK YANKEES	15
YOGI BERRA • NEW YORK YANKEES	12
DUKE SNIDER • BROOKLYN/ LOS ANGELES DODGERS	11
LOU GEHRIG • NEW YORK YANKEES	10
REGGIE JACKSON • OAKLAND A'S/ NEW YORK YANKEES	10

New York Yankees legend Mickey Mantle

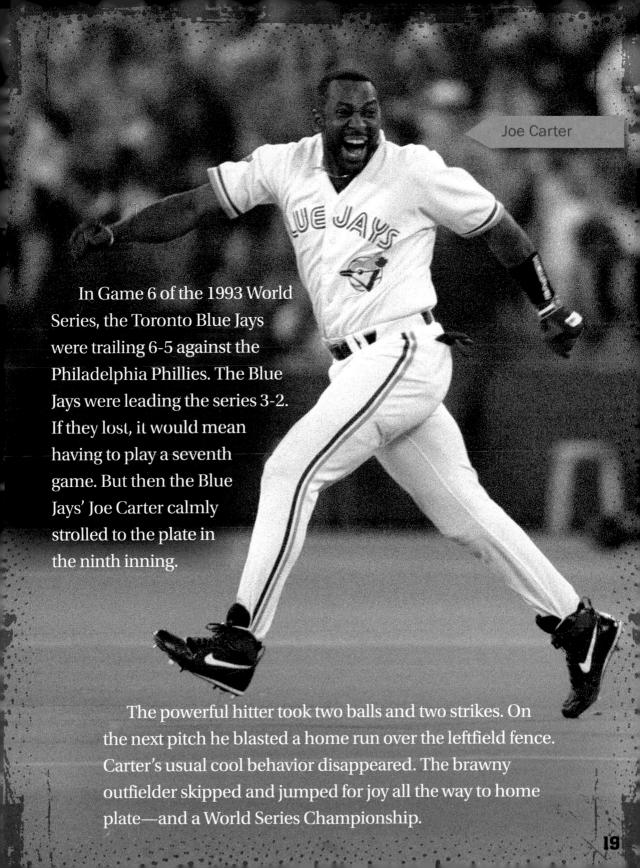

Joe Carter

In Game 6 of the 1993 World Series, the Toronto Blue Jays were trailing 6-5 against the Philadelphia Phillies. The Blue Jays were leading the series 3-2. If they lost, it would mean having to play a seventh game. But then the Blue Jays' Joe Carter calmly strolled to the plate in the ninth inning.

The powerful hitter took two balls and two strikes. On the next pitch he blasted a home run over the leftfield fence. Carter's usual cool behavior disappeared. The brawny outfielder skipped and jumped for joy all the way to home plate—and a World Series Championship.

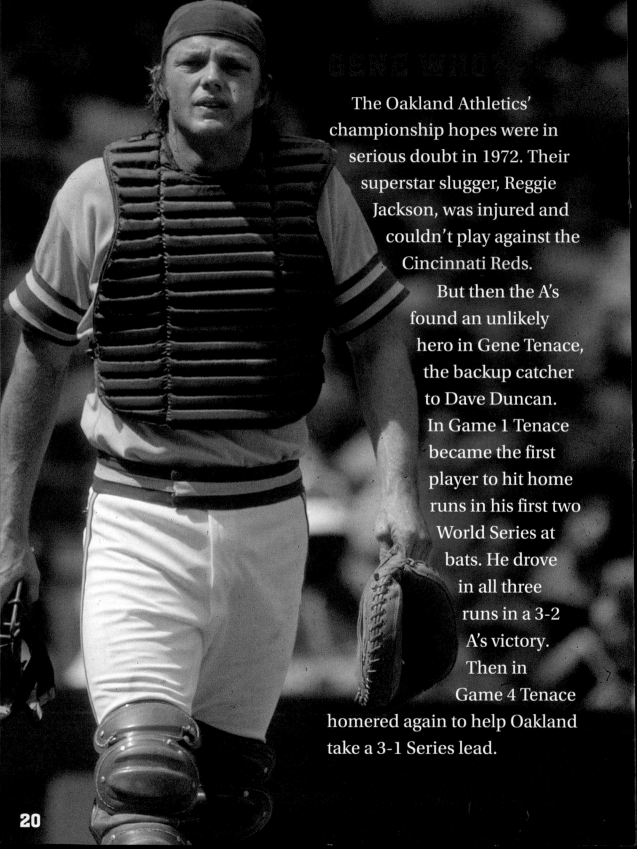

The Oakland Athletics' championship hopes were in serious doubt in 1972. Their superstar slugger, Reggie Jackson, was injured and couldn't play against the Cincinnati Reds.

But then the A's found an unlikely hero in Gene Tenace, the backup catcher to Dave Duncan. In Game 1 Tenace became the first player to hit home runs in his first two World Series at bats. He drove in all three runs in a 3-2 A's victory. Then in Game 4 Tenace homered again to help Oakland take a 3-1 Series lead.

But it wasn't over yet. Cincinnati stormed back and pushed the series to Game 7. In the final game Tenace sealed his place in history. He batted in two runs and led the A's to win the championship. Tenace finished the World Series with four home runs and nine runs batted in (RBIs). No other A's player had more than one RBI during the series. Tenace's four home runs tied the record at that time held by Babe Ruth and Lou Gehrig. Tenace was the clear choice for the 1972 World Series Most Valuable Player (MVP) award.

SERIES SLUGGERS

Little adds more drama than when a player hits a big shot over the fence. Some sluggers have hit several home runs in a single World Series. In 2009 the Philadelphia Phillies' Chase Utley slammed five homers over the wall. Reggie Jackson also smacked five home runs for the New York Yankees in 1977. Through the years, eight other players have hit four homers in a World Series.

Chase Utley

The Greatest Moments

The greatest World Series moments stick in fans' memories forever. Some of these moments have turned certain defeat into victory. Some have ruined the reputations of great baseball players. Others are simply another glorious story about a legendary player. But they all have one thing in common—they are all unforgettable.

WILLIE'S BASKET CATCH

With 111 wins, the 1954 Cleveland Indians set a league record for regular season victories. No one gave the New York Giants much of a chance against the Indians in the World Series. But with one amazing play, Giants centerfielder Willie Mays knocked the wind out of Cleveland's mighty Indians.

In Game 1 the two teams were locked in a tie in the eighth inning. Cleveland had two runners on base when their best hitter, Vic Wertz, came up to bat. Wertz already had three hits in the game. On the first pitch Wertz blasted the ball 450 feet into centerfield.

But Mays fiercely ran back to make an incredible basket catch over his shoulder. Then he stopped, spun around, and fired the ball to the infield to keep the Indians from scoring.

The Giants went on to win the game in extra innings. The loss stunned the Indians. The Giants caught fire and cruised to a World Series **sweep**.

sweep—when a team wins a series without losing a game

THE CALLED SHOT

In the 1932 World Series, the Chicago Cubs were outmatched by the New York Yankees. But when it came to trash talking, the Cubs were world-class opponents. Their favorite target was Babe Ruth.

In the 1932 World Series, Babe Ruth silenced his critics with two big home runs in Game 3.

In the fifth inning of Game 3, the trash talking hit a high point. The Cubs had tied the game, and Ruth was at the plate. The crowd at Wrigley Field showered him with boos and insults as he took two strikes.

Stories differ about what happened next. Some say Ruth pointed at the Cubs' bench because he was tired of the insults. Some say he pointed at the pitcher. Ruth himself said that he just pointed toward centerfield and said, "I'm gonna hit the next pitched ball right past the flagpole."

But there's no denying what happened after that. Ruth slammed the next pitch into the centerfield bleachers. As he trotted around the bases, he happily returned all the trash talking that had been hurled at him earlier. The Yankees went on to sweep the Cubs and win the championship.

Babe Ruth

THE CURSE OF THE BAMBINO

By 1918 the Boston Red Sox had won five World Series championships. But in 1920 Boston made a huge mistake. They sold Babe Ruth, "The Great Bambino," to the New York Yankees. The Red Sox didn't win another championship until 2004. Many believed the Red Sox were cursed by that horrible mistake, which became known as the "Curse of the Bambino."

Bill Buckner

BUCKNER'S FOLLY

The World Series has seen many big plays through the years. But Bill Buckner would like people to forget his memorable moment from the 1986 Series.

In Game 6 the Boston Red Sox were ahead of the New York Mets 5-3. In the 10th inning, Boston was one out away from their first title in 68 years. But then the team fell apart.

The Mets hit three straight singles and scored a run. Another run came through on a wild pitch. With the game tied, the Mets' Mookie Wilson hit a slow ground ball toward Buckner at first base. The ball squirted through Buckner's legs, allowing the Mets to score the winning run. The Mets went on to win Game 7 and the championship.

The Boston Red Sox were stunned after losing the 1986 World Series.

Several players could have been blamed for the loss, but Buckner's **error** was singled out. Coldhearted fans pelted him with insults. The Red Sox traded him the next year. But three years later the Red Sox brought Buckner back. In his first game, the fans seemed to forgive Buckner as they greeted him with a standing ovation.

error—when a player misses or drops the ball during a defensive play

The Los Angeles Dodgers made a fantastic run to the 1988 World Series. Veteran slugger Kirk Gibson was a big part of their success. But when they got to the World Series, Gibson was suffering from several injuries. Nobody thought he would play against the heavily favored Oakland Athletics.

During Game 1, Gibson stayed in the training room. He watched the game on TV as the A's built a 4-3 lead. In the ninth inning, the Dodgers were down to their last out. The A's star closer, Dennis Eckersley, was on the mound. Dodgers manager Tommy Lasorda needed a miracle. With a runner on first, Lasorda called on Gibson to pinch-hit.

Kirk Gibson

· WORLD SERIES APPEARANCES ·

NEW YORK YANKEES	40
LOS ANGELES DODGERS	18
SAN FRANCISCO GIANTS	18
ST. LOUIS CARDINALS	18
OAKLAND ATHLETICS	14

Eckersley immediately zipped in two fastballs, which Gibson hit foul. Before Gibson knew it, he was down in the **count** 0-2. He looked overmatched. But Gibson somehow worked the count to 3-2. On the next pitch, he smacked the ball over the rightfield wall. Gibson pumped his fist while limping around the bases for the Dodgers' win. It was his only at bat of the series. Gibson's home run knocked the life out of the A's. His heroics sparked the Dodgers to win the World Series four games to one.

Dennis Eckersley

count—the number of balls and strikes taken by the batter

GLOSSARY

count (KOUNT)—the number of balls and strikes on the batter at any time

error (AIR-uhr)—when a defensive player makes a mistake while fielding the ball

ground rule (GROUND ROOL)—a rule that applies to an individual baseball park; if a fair ball can't be played by a fielder, ground rules determine the number of bases the batter is awarded

pennant (PEN-uhnt)—a triangular flag that symbolizes a league championship

perfect game (PUR-fikt GAME)—a game in which a pitcher doesn't allow a single batter to reach first base

sweep (SWEEP)—when a team wins all the games in a series without losing to the opposing team

walk-off home run (WALK-off HOME RUN)—a game-winning home run in the bottom half of the last inning of a game

wild card (WILD CARD)—a team that advances to the playoffs without winning a division

READ MORE

Buckley, James. *Baseball.* DK Eyewitness Books. New York: DK Pub., 2010.

Doeden, Matt. *The Greatest Baseball Records.* Sports Records. Mankato, Minn.: Capstone Press, 2009.

LeBoutillier, Nate. *The Ultimate Guide to Pro Baseball Teams.* Ultimate Pro Guides. Mankato, Minn.: Capstone Press, 2011.

INTERNET SITES

FactHound offers a safe, fun way to find Internet sites related to this book. All of the sites on FactHound have been researched by our staff.

Here's all you do:

Visit *www.facthound.com*

Type in this code: 9781429665742

Check out projects, games and lots more at
www.capstonekids.com

INDEX